The
LITTLE
BLACK
BOOK
of

CHORDS

over
1100
GUITAR
CHORDS

ISBN: 978-1-78038-799-4

EXCLUSIVELY DISTRIBUTED BY

HAL•LEONARD®

Visit Hal Leonard Online at
www.halleonard.com

World headquarters, contact:
Hal Leonard
777 West Bluemound Road
Milwaukee, WI 53213
Email: info@halleonard.com

In Europe, contact:
Hal Leonard Europe Limited
1 Red Place
London, W1K 6PL
Email: info@halleonardeurope.com

In Australia, contact:
Hal Leonard Australia Pty. Ltd.
4 Lentara Court
Cheltenham, Victoria, 3192 Australia
Email: info@halleonard.com.au

THE CHORD DIAGRAM

The chords are displayed as diagrams that represent the fingerboard of the guitar. In this book there are six vertical lines representing the six strings of the guitar. Horizontal lines represent the frets. The strings are arranged with the high E (first, or thinnest) string to the right, and the low E (sixth, or thickest) to the left. The black circles indicate at which fret the finger is to be placed and the number tells you which finger to use. At the top of the diagram there is a thick black line indicating the nut of the guitar. Diagrams for chords up the neck just have a fret line at the top with a Roman numeral to the right to identify the first fret of the diagram. Above the chord diagram you will occasionally see **X**'s and **O**'s. An **X** indicates that the string below it is either not played or damped, an **O** simply means the string is played as an open string. At the bottom of the diagram are the note names that make up the chord. This information can be helpful when making up lead licks or chord solos. A curved line tells you to barre the strings with the finger shown; that is, lay your finger flat across the indicated strings.

The fingerings in this book might be different from fingerings you have encountered on other chord books. They were chosen for their overall practicality in the majority of situations.

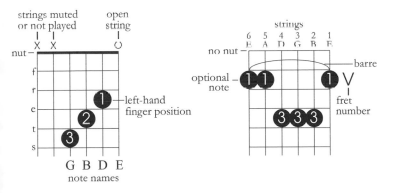

3

ALTERNATE CHORD NAMES

This chord encyclopedia uses a standard chord naming approach, but when playing from sheet music or using other music books, you will find alternative chord names or symbols. Below is a chart by which you can cross reference alternative names and symbols with the ones used in this book.

Chord Symbol	Chord Name	Alternate Name or Symbol
	major	M; Maj
m	minor	m; min; -
6	sixth	major6; Maj6; M6
m6	minor sixth	minor6; m6; min6; -6
6/9	six nine	6(add9); Maj6(add9); M6(add9)
maj7	major seventh	major7; M7; Maj7; Δ7
7	dominant seventh	dominant seventh; dom
7♭5	seventh flat five	7(♭5); 7(-5)
7♯5	seventh sharp five	+7; 7(+5); aug7
m7	minor seventh	minor seven; m7; min7; -7
m(maj7)	minor with a major seventh	minor(major7); m(M7); min(Maj7); major7; m(+7); -(M7); min(addM7)
m7♭5	minor seventh flat five	°7; ½dim; ½dim7; m7(♭5); m7(-5)
°7	diminished seventh	°; dim; dim7
9	ninth	7(add9)
9♭5	ninth flat five	9(♭5); 9(-5)
9♯5	ninth sharp five	+9; 9(+5); aug9
maj9	major ninth	major 9; M9; Δ9; Maj7(add9); M7(add9)
m9	minor ninth	minor9; m9; min9
m11	minor eleventh	minor11; m11; min11
13	thirteenth	7(add13); 7(add6)
maj13	major thirteen	major13; M13; Δ13; Maj7(add13); M7(add13); M7(add6)
m13	minor thirteen	minor13; m13; -13; min7(add13); m7(add13); -7(add13)
sus4	suspended fourth	(sus4)

C

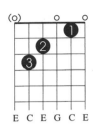

E C E G C E

G C E G C E

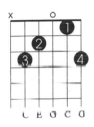

C E G C E

G C G C E C

G C E C

V

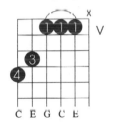

C E G C E

V

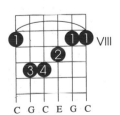

C G C E G C

VIII

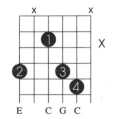

E C G C

X

5

C

Csus4

F G C G

G C F C F G — III

C G C F G C — VIII

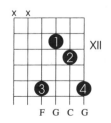

F G C G — XII

C6

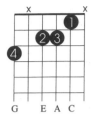

G E A C

C G C E A

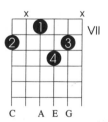

C A E G — VII

C G E A C — VIII

6

C6/9

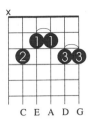

C E A D G

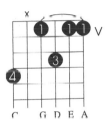
V

C G D E A

VII

E A D G C

IX

G C E A D

Cmaj7

C E G B E

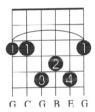

G C G B E G

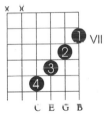
VII

C E G B

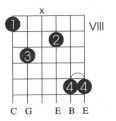
VIII

C G   E B E

C

Cmaj9

C G B D E

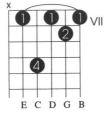

VII

E C D G B

Cmaj13

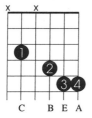

C B E A

VII

C E A D G B

Cm

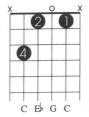

C E♭ G C

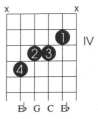

IV

E♭ G C E♭

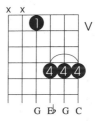

V

G E♭ G C

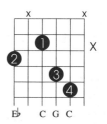

X

E♭ C G C

8

Cm

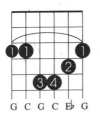

G C G C E♭ G

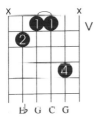

E♭ G C G
V

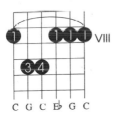

C G C E♭ G C
VIII

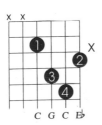

C G C E♭
X

Cm6

A E♭ G C G

C A E♭ G

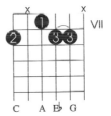

C A E♭ G
VII

C G C E♭ A C
VIII

C

Cm7

Eb Bb C G

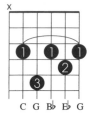

C G Bb Eb G

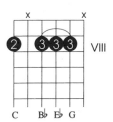

VIII

C Bb Eb G

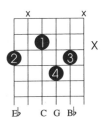

X

Eb C G Bb

Cm(maj7)

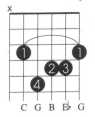

C G B Eb G

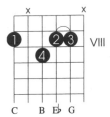

VIII

C B Eb G

Cm9

C Eb Bb D

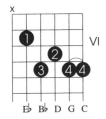

VI

Eb Bb D G C

Cm11

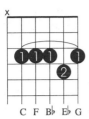

C F B♭ E♭ G

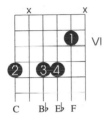

VI

C B♭ E♭ F

Cm13

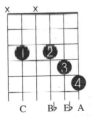

C B♭ E♭ A

VIII

C G B♭ E♭ A C

Cm7♭5

C G♭ B♭ E♭

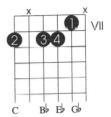

VII

C B♭ E♭ G♭

C°7

V

B♭♭ E♭ A C G♭ B♭♭

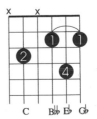

C B♭♭ E♭ G♭

C

C7

G C E B♭ C E

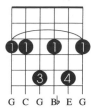

G C G B♭ E G

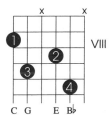

C G E B♭

VIII

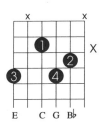

E C G B♭

X

C7

C G B♭ E G C

VIII

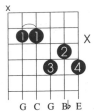

G C G B♭ E

X

C7sus4

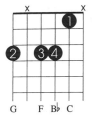

G F B♭ C

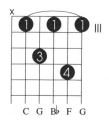

C G B♭ F G

III

C7♭5

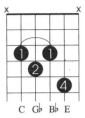

C G♭ B♭ E

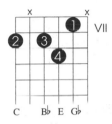

VII

C B♭ E G♭

C7♯5

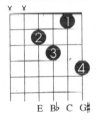

E B♭ C G♯

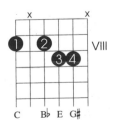

VIII

C B♭ E G♯

C9

C E B♭ D G

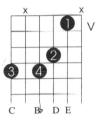

V

C B♭ D E

VIII

C G B♭ E G D

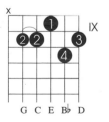

IX

G C E B♭ D

C

C9sus4

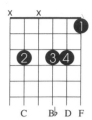

x · x
① ② ③④

C B♭ D F

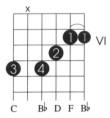

x
① ① VI
② ③ ④

C B♭ D F B♭

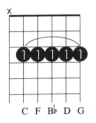

x
① ① ① ① ①

C F B♭ D G

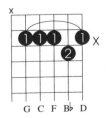

x
① ① ① ① X
②

G C F B♭ D

C9♭5

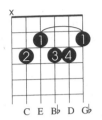

x
① ①
② ③④

C E B♭ D G♭

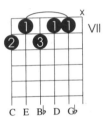

① ① ① ① VII
② ③

C E B♭ D G♭

C9♯5

○ · ○ · ○
① ② ③

E B♭ D G♯ C E

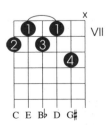

① ① VII
② ③
④

C E B♭ D G♯

14

C13

B♭ E A C

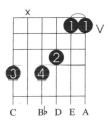

C B♭ D E A

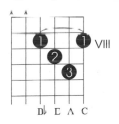

D♭ E A C

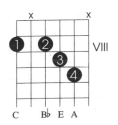

C B♭ E A

15

C#

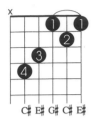

C# E# G# C# E#

G# E# G# C#

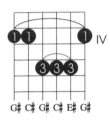

IV

G# C# G# C# E# G#

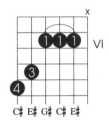

VI

C# E# G# C# E#

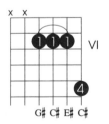

VI

G# C# E# C#

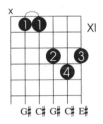

XI

G# C# G# C# E#

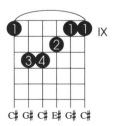

IX

C# G# C# E# G# C#

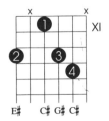

XI

E# C# G# C#

C#sus4

G# C# F# C# F# G#

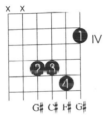

x x

G# C# F# G#

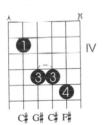

IV

C# G# C# F#

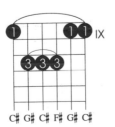

IX

C# G# C# F# G# C#

C#6

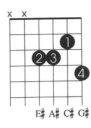

x x

E# A# C# G#

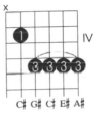

x

IV

C# G# C# E# A#

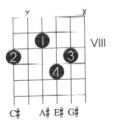

VIII

C#   A# E# G#

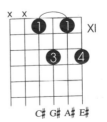

x x

XI

C# G# A# E#

C#

C#6/9

A# D# G# C# E#

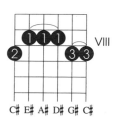
VI

C# G# D# E# A#

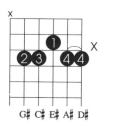
VIII

C# E# A# D# G# C#

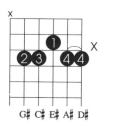
X

G# C# E# A# D#

C#maj7

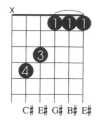

C# E# G# B# E#

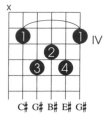
IV

C# G# B# E# G#

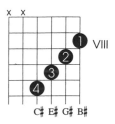
VIII

C# E# G# B#

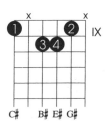
IX

C# B# E# G#

18

C#maj9

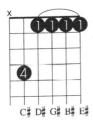

C# D# G# B# E#

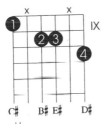

IX

C# B# E# D#

C#maj13

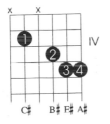

IV

C# B# F# A#

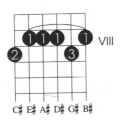

VIII

C# E# A# D# G# B#

C#m

C# E G# C#

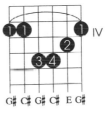

IV

G# C# G# C# E G#

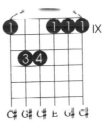

IX

C# G# C# E G# C#

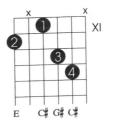

XI

E C# G# C#

C#m

C#m6

E G# C# E

C# E A# C# G#

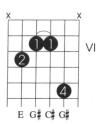

VI

E G# C# G#

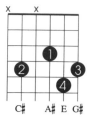

C# A# E G#

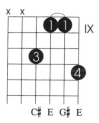

IX

C# E G# E

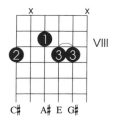

VIII

C# A# E G#

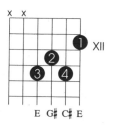

XII

E G# C# E

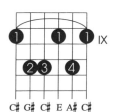

IX

C# G# C# E A# C#

C#m7

C# E G# B E

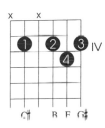

C# B E G#

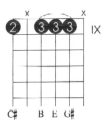

C# B E G#

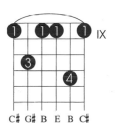

C# G# B E B C#

C#m(maj7)

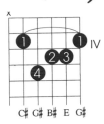

C# G# B# E G#

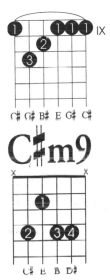

C# G# B# E G# C#

C#m9

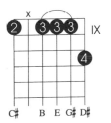

C# E B D#

C# B E G# D#

C#m11

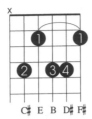

C# E B D# F#

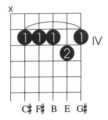

IV

C# F# B E G#

C#m13

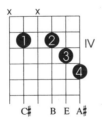

IV

C#　　B E A#

IX

C# G# B E A# C#

C#m7♭5

B E G C# E

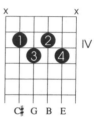

IV

C# G B E

C#°7

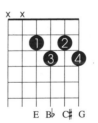

E B♭ C# G

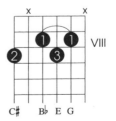

VIII

C#　B♭ E G

C#7

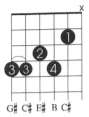

G# C# E# B C#

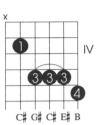

C# G# C# E# B

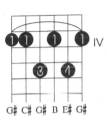

IV

G# C# G# B E# G#

XI

G# C# G# B# E#

C#7sus4

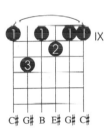

IX

C# G# B E# G# C#

G# F# B C#

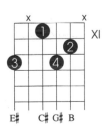

XI

E# C# G# B

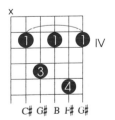

IV

C# G# B F# G#

C#7b5

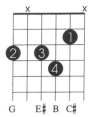

G E# B C#

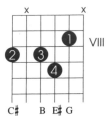
VIII

C# B E# G

C#7#5

C# E# G⁝ B

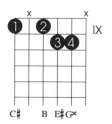
IX

C# B E#G⁝

C#9

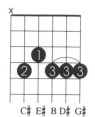

C# E# B D# G#

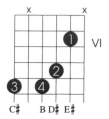
VI

C# B D# E#

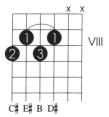
VIII

C# E# B D#

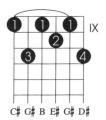
IX

C# G# B E# G# D#

24

C#9sus4

C# B D# F#

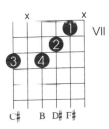

VII

C# B D# F#

IV

C# F# B D# G#

XI

G# C# F# B D#

C#9b5

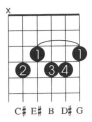

C# E# B D# G

VIII

C# E# B D# G

C#9#5

C# E# B D# G×

VIII

C# E# B D# G×

C#

C#13

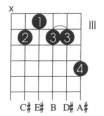

III

C# E# B D# A#

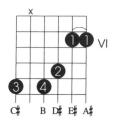

VI

C# B D# E# A#

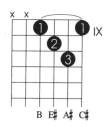

IX

B E# A# C#

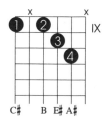

IX

C# B E# A#

D

A D A F#

D F# A D F#

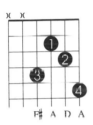

F# A D A

A D A D F# A V

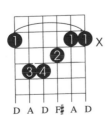

D F# A D F# VII

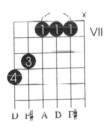

A D F# D VII

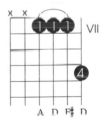

D A D F# A D X

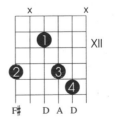

F# D A D XII

Dsus4

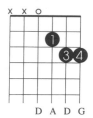

D A D G

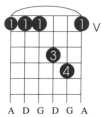

A D G D G A

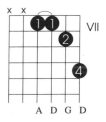

A D G D

D A D G A D

D6

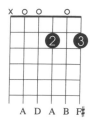

A D A B F#

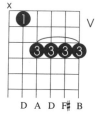

D A D F# B

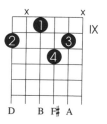

D B F# A

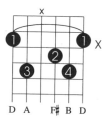

D A F# B D

D

D6/9

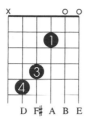

D F# A B E

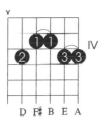

IV

D F# B E A

VII

D   A E F# B

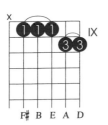

IX

F# B E A D

Dmaj7

D F# A C# F#

V

D A C# F# A

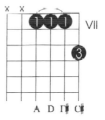

VII

A D F# C#

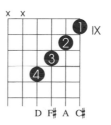

IX

D F# A C#

D

Dmaj9

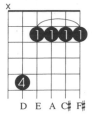

D E A C♯ F♯

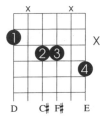

X

D C♯ F♯ E

Dmaj13

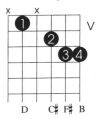

V

D C♯ F♯ B

IX

D F♯ B E A C♯

Dm

A D A D F

V

A D A D F A

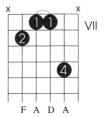

VII

F A D A

X

D A D F A D

Dm

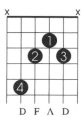

D F A D

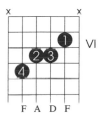

VI

F A D F

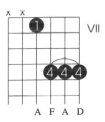

VII

A F A D

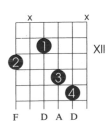

XII

F D A D

Dm6

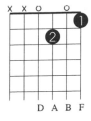

D A B F

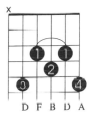

D F B D A

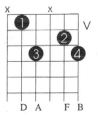

V

D A F B

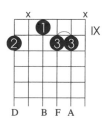

IX

D B F A

D

31

Dm7　Dm(maj7)

D

D A C F

D A C# F

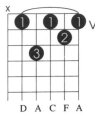

D A C F A

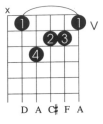

D A C# F A

Dm9

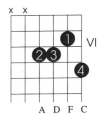

A D F C

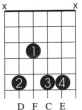

D F C E

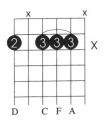

D C F A

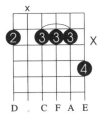

D C F A E

Dm11

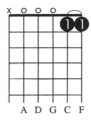

A D G C F

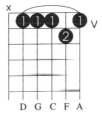

V

D G C F A

Dm7♭5

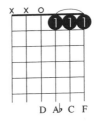

D A♭ C F

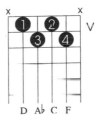

V

D A♭ C F

Dm13

A D B C F

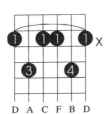

X

D A C F B D

D°7

D A♭ C♭ F

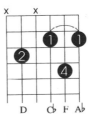

D C♭ F A♭

D

D7

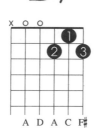

A D A C F#

III

A D F# C D

V

A D A C F# A

X

D A C F# A D

D7

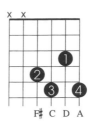

F# C D A

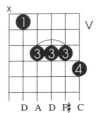

V

D A D F# C

D7sus4

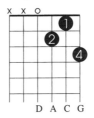

D A C G

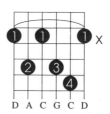

X

D A C G C D

D7♭5

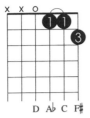

D A♭ C F♯

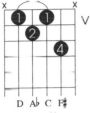

V

D A♭ C F♯

D7♯5

D A♯ C F♯

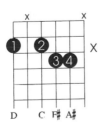

D   C F♯ A♯

D9

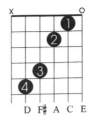

D F♯ A C E

D F♯ C E A

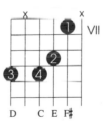

VII

D   C E F♯

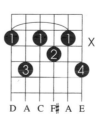

X

D A C F♯ A E

D

D9sus4

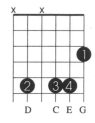

D C E G

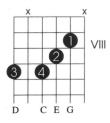

VIII

D C E G

V

D G C E A

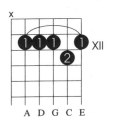

XII

A D G C E

D9♭5

IV

D F♯ C E A♭

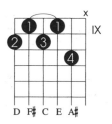

IX

D F♯ C E A♭

D9♯5

F♯ C E A♯ D F♯

IX

D F♯ C E A♯

36

D13

D

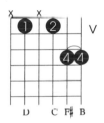

C F# B D

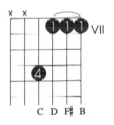

V

D C F# B

VII

C D F# B

X

D C F# B E

E♭

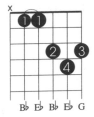

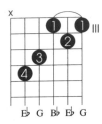

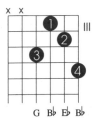

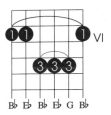

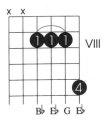

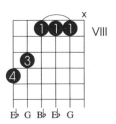

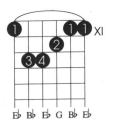

E♭sus4

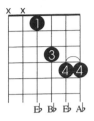

Eb Bb Eb Ab

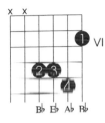

Bb Eb Ab Bb — VI

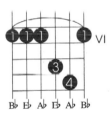

Bb Eb Ab Eb Ab Bb — VI

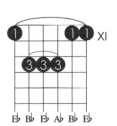

Eb Bb Eb Ab Bb Eb — XI

E♭6

Eb Bb C G

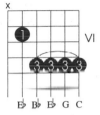

Eb Bb Eb G C — VI

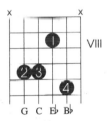

G C Eb Bb — VIII

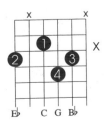

Eb C G Bb — X

E♭

39

E♭6/9　　E♭maj7

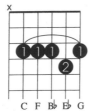

C F B♭ E♭ G

E♭ B♭ D G

E♭

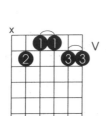

V

E♭ G C F B♭

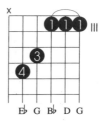

III

E♭ G B♭ D G

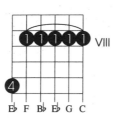

VIII

E♭ F B♭ E♭ G C

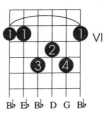

VI

B♭ E♭ B♭ D G B♭

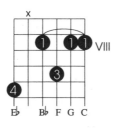

VIII

E♭ B♭ F G C

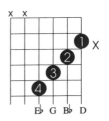

X

E♭ G B♭ D

E♭maj9

Eb G D F

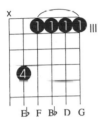

III

E♭ F B♭ D G

E♭maj13

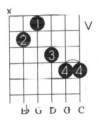

V

E♭ G D C♭ C

X

E♭ G C F B♭ D

E♭m

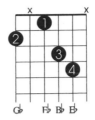

G♭ F♭ B♭ E♭

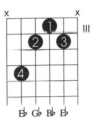

III

E♭ G♭ B♭ E♭

E♭

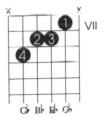

VII

C♭ B♭ E♭ G♭

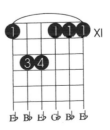

XI

E♭ B♭ E♭ G♭ B♭ E♭

E♭m   E♭m6

B♭ G♭ B♭ E♭

E♭ B♭ C G♭

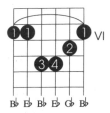

E♭

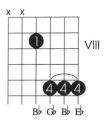

VI

B♭ E♭ B♭ E♭ G♭ B♭

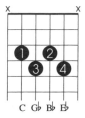

C G♭ B♭ E♭

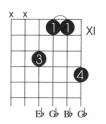

VIII

B♭ G♭ B♭ E♭

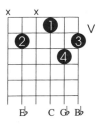

V

E♭   C G♭ B♭

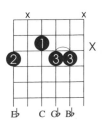

XI

E♭ G♭ B♭ G♭

X

E♭   C G♭ B♭

E♭m7

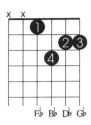

Fb Bb Db Gb

Db Gb Bb Db

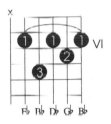
VI

Fb Bb Db Gb Bb

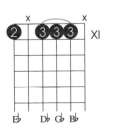
XI

Eb Db Gb Bb

E♭m(maj7)

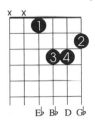

Eb Bb D Gb

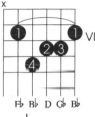
VI

Fb Bb D Gb Bb

E♭m9

Gb Eb Bb Db F

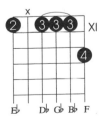
XI

Eb Db Gb Bb F

Ebm11

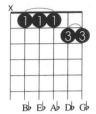

Bb Eb Ab Db Gb

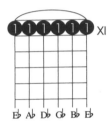

Eb Ab Db Gb Bb Eb — XI

Ebm7b5

Eb Bb Db Gb

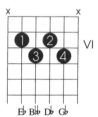

Eb Bb Db Gb — VI

Eb

Ebm13

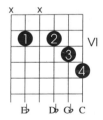

Eb Db Gb C — VI

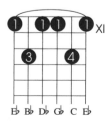

Eb Bb Db Gb C Eb — XI

Eb°7

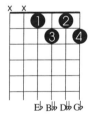

Eb Bbb Dbb Gb

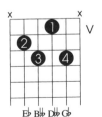

Eb Bbb Dbb Gb — V

E♭7

Eb Bb Db G

Db Bb Eb G

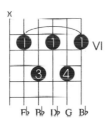

Fb Bb Db G Bb VI

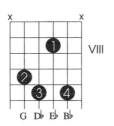

G Db Eb Bb VIII

E♭7

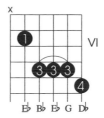

Eb Bb Eb G Db VI

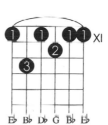

Eb Bb Db G Bb Eb XI

E♭

E♭7sus4

Bb Eb Ab Db

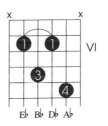

Eb Bb Db Ab VI

E♭7♭5

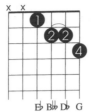

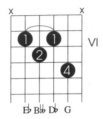

E♭ B♭♭ D♭ G

E♭ B♭♭ D♭ G — VI

E♭9

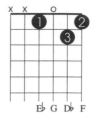

E♭ G D♭ F

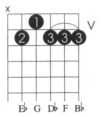

E♭ G D♭ F B♭ — V

E♭7♯5

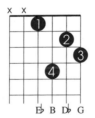

E♭ B D♭ G

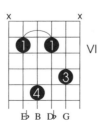

E♭ B D♭ G — VI

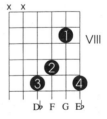

D♭ F G E♭ — VIII

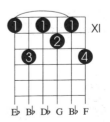

E♭ B♭ D♭ G B♭ F — XI

E♭

E♭9sus4

B♭ E♭ A♭ D♭ F

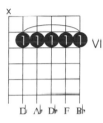

VI

D♭ A♭ D♭ F B♭

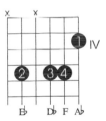

IV

E♭ D♭ F A♭

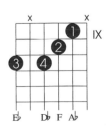

IX

E♭ D♭ F A♭

E♭9♭5

B♭♭ E♭ G D♭ F

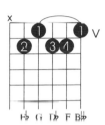

V

H♭ G D♭ F B♭♭

E♭9♯5

G D♭ F B E♭ G

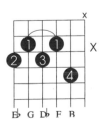

X

E♭ G D♭ F B

E♭13

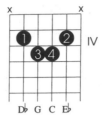

E♭

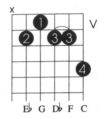

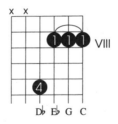

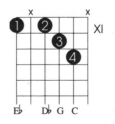

E

E B E G# B E

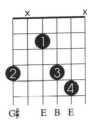

G#　E B E

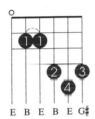

E B E B E G#

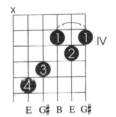

E G# B E G#

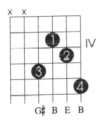

G# B E B

B E B E G# B

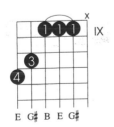

E G# B E G#

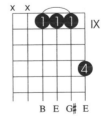

B E G# E

Esus4　　　E6

E B E A B E

E B E G# C# E

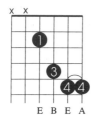

E B E A

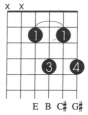

E B C# G#

VII

B E A E A B

VII

E B E G# C#

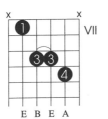

VII

E B E A

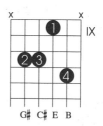

IX

G# C# E B

E

50

E6/9

E B   G# C# F#

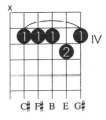

C# F# B E G#   IV

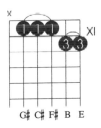

G# C# F# B E   XI

E G# C# F# B E   XI

Emaj7

E B D# G# B E

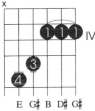

E G# B D# G#   IV

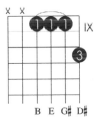

B E G# D#   IX

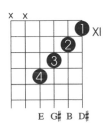

E G# B D#   XI

E

51

Emaj9

E B F♯ B D♯ G♯

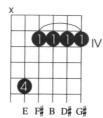

E F♯ B D♯ G♯ IV

Emaj13

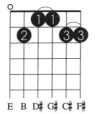

E B D♯ G♯ C♯ F♯

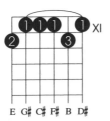

E G♯ C♯ F♯ B D♯ XI

Em

E B E G B E

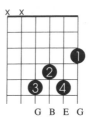

G B E G

B E B E G B VII

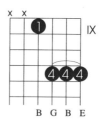

B G B E IX

E

Em

E B E G

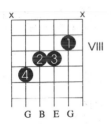

IV

E G B E

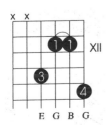

VIII

G B E G

XII

E G B G

Em6

E B E G C# E

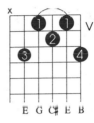

V

E G C# E B

E

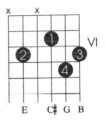

VI

E C# G B

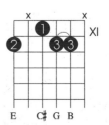

XI

E C# G B

Em7

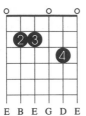

E B E G D E

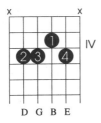

IV

D G B E

VII

E B D G

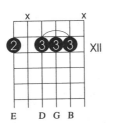

XII

E   D G B

Em(maj7)

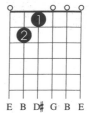

E B D♯ G B E

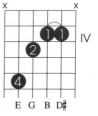

IV

E G B D♯

Em9

E B D G B F♯

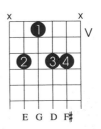

V

E G D F♯

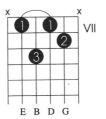

E

Em11

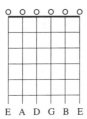

E A D G B E

VII

E A D G B

Em7♭5

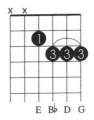

E B♭ D G

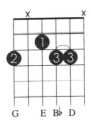

G   E B♭ D

Em13

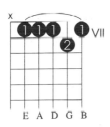

E B D G C♯ F♯

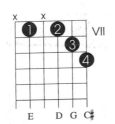
VII

E   D G C♯

E°7

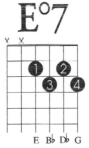

E B♭ D♭ G

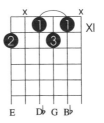
XI

E   D♭ G B♭

E7

E B D G# B E

E7

E B E G# D E

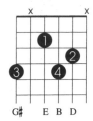

G#   E B D

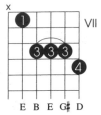 VII

E B E G# D

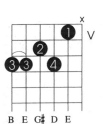 V

B E G# D E

E7sus4

B E A D

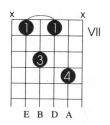 VII

B E B D G# B

 VII

E B D A

E

E7♭5

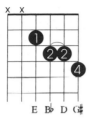

E B♭ D G♯

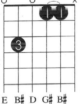

VII

E B♭ D G♯

E7♯5

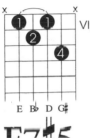

E B♯ D G♯ B♯

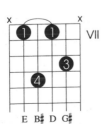

VII

E B♯ D G♯

E9

E B D G♯ B F♯

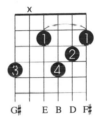

G♯ E B D F♯

E

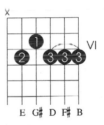

VI

E G♯ D F♯ B

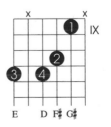

IX

E D F♯ G♯

E9sus4

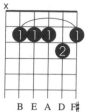

B E A D F#

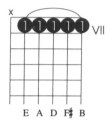
VII

E A D F# B

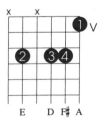
V

E D F# A

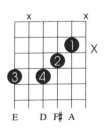
X

E D F# A

E9♭5

B♭ E G# D F#

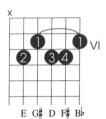
VI

E G# D F# B♭

E9♯5

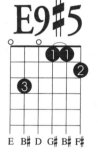

E B# D G# B# F#

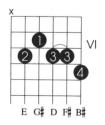
VI

E G# D F# B#

E

58

E13

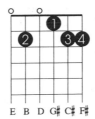

E B D G# C# F#

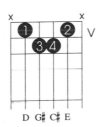

V

D G# C# E

E

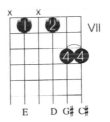

VII

E   D G# C#

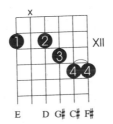

XII

E   D G# C# F#

59

F

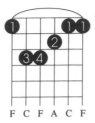

F C F A C F

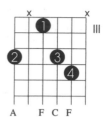

III

A   F C F

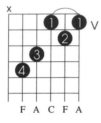

V

F A C F A

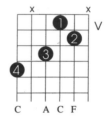

V

C   A C F

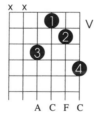

V

A C F C

VII

C F C F A C

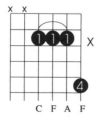

X

C F A F

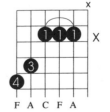

X

F A C F A

60

Fsus4

F C F B♭ C F

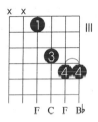

III

F C F B♭

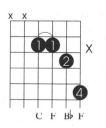

VIII

C F B♭ F B♭ C

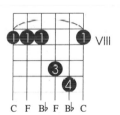

X

C F B♭ F

F6

x   x

F C   A D

x

C F C D A

x   x

VII

F C D A

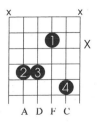

x   x

X

A D F C

F

F6/9

F C Å D G

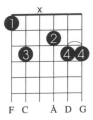

V

D G C F A

X

F G C F A D

XII

F A D G C F

Fmaj7

F E A C

F C E A

V

F A C E A

VIII

F C E A C

Fmaj9

F A E G C

F C G B A

Fmaj13

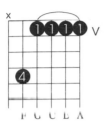

F E A D

F A D G C E

Fm

F C F A♭ C F

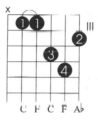

C F C F A♭

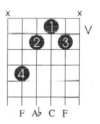

F A♭ C F

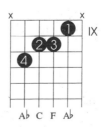

A♭ C F A♭

Fm

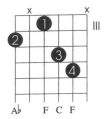

x   x

III

A♭   F   C   F

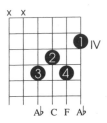

x   x

IV

A♭   C   F   A♭

VIII

C   F   C   F   A♭   C

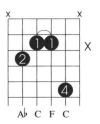

x   x

X

A♭   C   F   C

Fm6

x   x   o

D   A♭   C   F

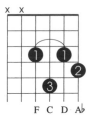

x   x

F   C   D   A♭

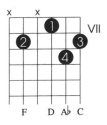

x   x

VII

F   D   A♭   C

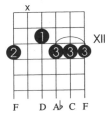

x

XII

F   D   A♭   C   F

F

Fm7

F C F A♭ E♭ F

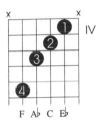

IV

F A♭ C E♭

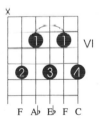

VI

F A♭ E♭ F C

VIII

F C E♭ A♭ C

Fm(maj7)

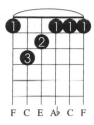

F C E A♭ C F

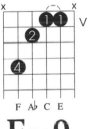

V

F A♭ C E

Fm9

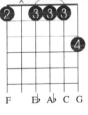

F E♭ A♭ C G

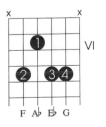

VI

F A♭ E♭ G

F

Fm11

F Bb Eb Ab C F

F Ab Eb G Bb

Fm7b5

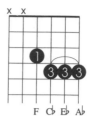

F Cb Eb Ab

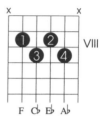
VIII

F Cb Eb Ab

Fm13

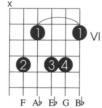

F C Eb Ab D F

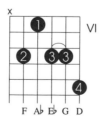
VI

F Ab Eb G D

F°7

F Cb Ebb Ab

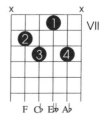
VII

F Cb Ebb Ab

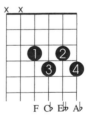

F

F7

F C E♭ A C F

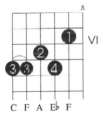

C F C E♭ A

VI

C F A E♭ F

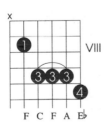
VIII

F C F A E♭

F7

F C   A E♭

VIII

C F C E♭ A C

F7sus4

F C E♭ B♭ C F

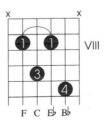
VIII

F C E♭ B♭

F7♭5

F   E♭ A C♭

F C♭ E♭ A   VIII

F7♯5

F   E♭ A C♯

F C♯ E♭ A   VIII

F9

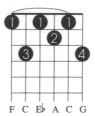

F C E♭ A C G

F A E♭ G C   VII

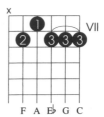

F   E♭ G A   X

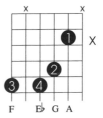

A E♭ G C F   XII

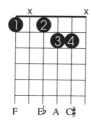

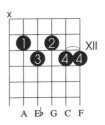

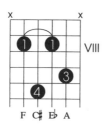

F9sus4

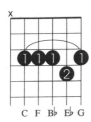

C F B♭ E♭ G

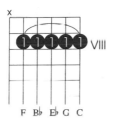

VIII

F B♭ E♭ G C

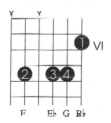

VI

F E♭ G B♭

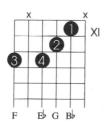

XI

F E♭ G B♭

F9♭5

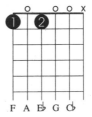

F A E♭ G C♭

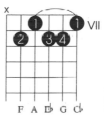

VII

F A E♭ G C♭

F9♯5

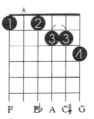

F E♭ A C♯ G

VII

F A E♭ G C♯

F

F13

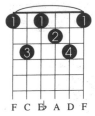

F C E♭ A D F

VII

F A E♭ G D

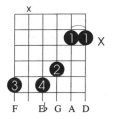

X

F E♭ G A D

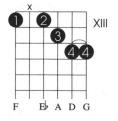

XIII

F E♭ A D G

70

F# C# F# A# C# F#

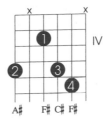

A#   F# C# F#

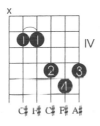

C# F# C# F# A#

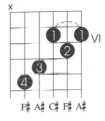

F# A# C# F# A#

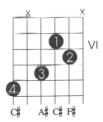

C#   A# C# F#

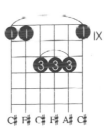

C# F# C# F# A# C#

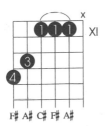

F# A# C# F# A#

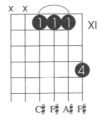

C# F# A# F#

F#sus4

F#6

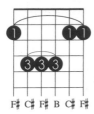

F# C# F# B C# F#

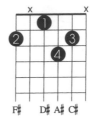

F#   D# A# C#

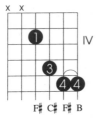

IV

F# C# F# B

F# C#   A# D#

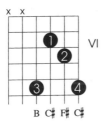

VI

B C# F# C#

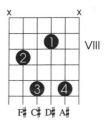

VIII

F# C# D# A#

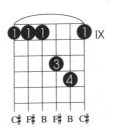

IX

C# F# B F# B C#

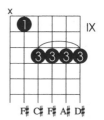

IX

F# C# F# A# D#

F#

F#6/9

F#maj7

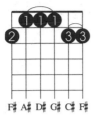

F# A# D# G# C# F#

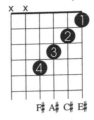

F# A# C# E#

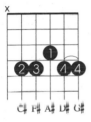

C# F# A# D# G#

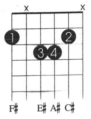

F#   E# A# C#

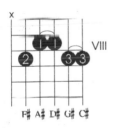

VIII

F# A# D# G# C#

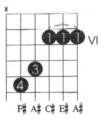

VI

F# A# C# E# A#

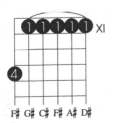

XI

F# G# C# F# A# D#

IX

C# F# C# E# A# C#

F#maj9

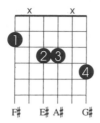

F# E# A# G#

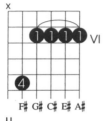
VI

F# G# C# E# A#

F#m

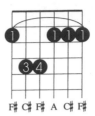

F# C# F# A C# F#

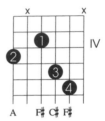
IV

A F# C# F#

F#

F#maj13

F# A# D# G# C# E#

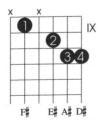
IX

F# E# A# D#

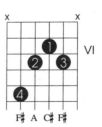
VI

F# A C# F#

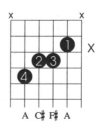
X

A C# F# A

74

F#m

F# A C# A

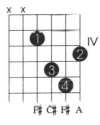

IV

F# C# F# A

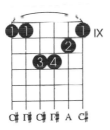

IX

C# D# C# D# A C#

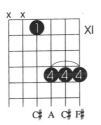

XI

C# A C# F#

F#m6

F# D# A C# F#

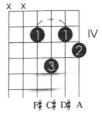

IV

F# C# D# A

VII

F# A D# F# C#

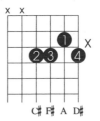

X

C# F# A D#

F#m7　F#m(maj7)

F#　E　A　C#

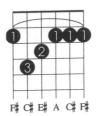

F#　C#　E#　A　C#　F#

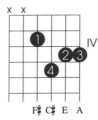

F#　C#　E　A

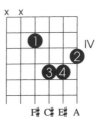

F#　C#　E#　A

F#

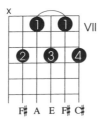

F#　A　E　F#　C#

F#m9

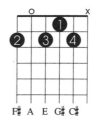

F#　A　E　G#　C#

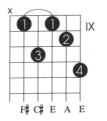

F#　C#　E　A　E

F#　A　E　G#

76

F#m11

F# B E A C# F#

IX

F# B E A C#

F#m13

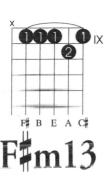

F# C# E A D# F#

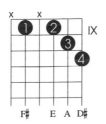
IX

F# E A D#

F#m7b5

E A C F#

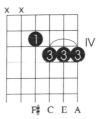
IV

F# C E A

F#°7

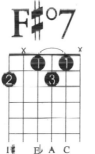

F# Eb A C

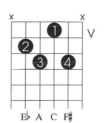
V

Eb A C F#

F#

F#7

F# A# C# E

F# C#　A# E

IV

C# F# C# E A#

IX

C# F# C# E A# C#

F#7

F# C# E A# C# F#

IX

F# C# F# A# E

F#7sus4

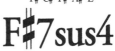

F# C# E B C# F#

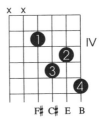

IV

F# C# E B

78

F#7b5

F#   E   A#   C

C   A#   E   F#

F#7#5

F#   E   A#   C×

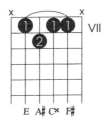

E   A#   C×   F#

F#9

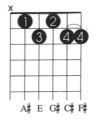

A#   E   G#   C#   F#

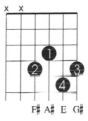

F#   A#   E   G#

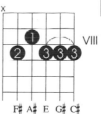

F#   A#   E   G#   C#

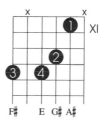

F#   E   G#   A#

F#

F#9sus4

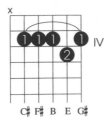

x

① ① ① ① IV
   ②

C# F# B E G#

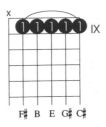

x

① ① ① ① ① IX

F# B E G# C#

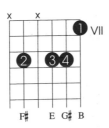

x x

       ① VII
 ② ③④

F# E G# B

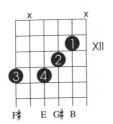

x   x

    ① XII
  ②
③ ④

F# E G# B

F#9♭5

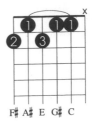

x

 ① ① ①
② ③

F# A# E G# C

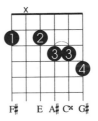

x

 ①   ① VIII
② ③④

F# A# E G# C

F#9#5

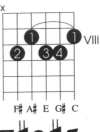

x

① ②
   ③③
    ④

F# E A# C× G#

x

 ①
② ③③ VIII
   ④

F# A# E G# C×

F#

F#13

E A# D# F#

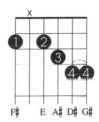

F# E A# D# G#

F# C# E A# D# F#

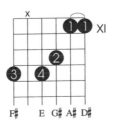

F# E G# A# D#

81

G

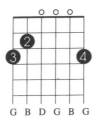

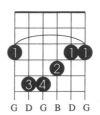

G B D G B G

G D G B D G

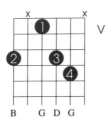

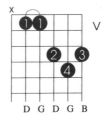

B G D G

D G D G B

V

V

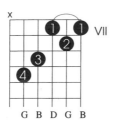

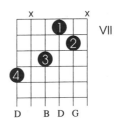

G B D G B

D B D G

VII

VII

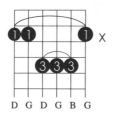

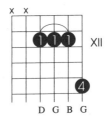

D G D G B G

D G B G

X

XII

Gsus4

G D G C D G

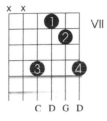

VII

C D G D

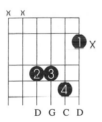

X

D G C D

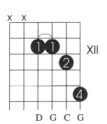

XII

D G C G

G6

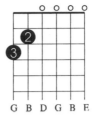

G B D G B E

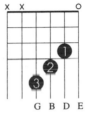

G B D E

G D   B E G

G

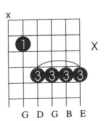

X

G D G B E

83

G6/9

G B E A D G

G D B E A

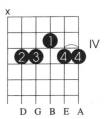

IV

D G B E A

VII

E A D G B

Gmaj7

G B D G B F#

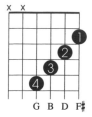

G B D F#

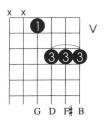

V

G D F# B

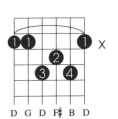

X

D G D F# B D

G

84

Gmaj9

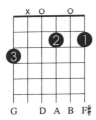

G   D A B F#

VII

G A D F# B

Gmaj13

G B E A D F#

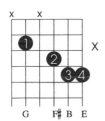

X

G   F# B E

Gm

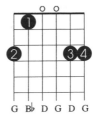

G B♭ D G D G

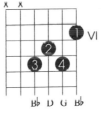

III

G B♭ D B♭

VI

B♭ D G B♭

G

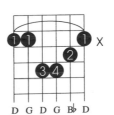

X

D G D G B♭ D

Gm

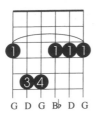

G D G B♭ D G

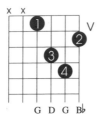

V

G D G B♭

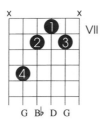

VII

G B♭ D G

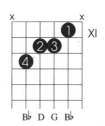

XI

B♭ D G B♭

Gm6

E B♭ D G

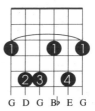

G D G B♭ E G

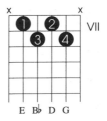

VII

E B♭ D G

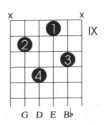

IX

G D E B♭

G

Gm7

x   o   x

Bb F G D

x   x

G F Bb D

III

G D F Bb F G

x   x

G F Bb D

Gm(maj7)

G D F# Bb D G

x   x   VII

G Bb D F#

Gm9

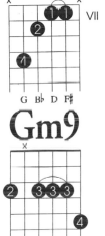

x

G F Bb D A

G

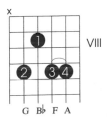

x

VIII

G Bb F A

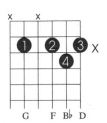

87

Gm11

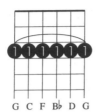

G C F B♭ D G

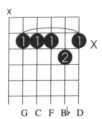

G C F B♭ D

Gm7♭5

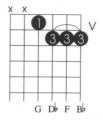

G D♭ F B♭

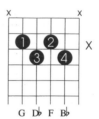

G D♭ F B♭

Gm13

G D F B♭ E G

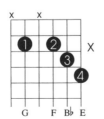

G F B♭ E

G°7

G F♭ B♭ D♭

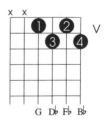

G D♭ F♭ B♭

G7

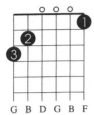

G B D G B F

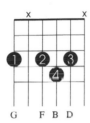

G   F B D

G D F B D G

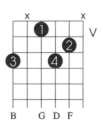

B   G D F

G7

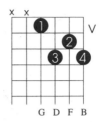

G D F B

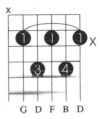

G D F B D

G7sus4

G D F C D G

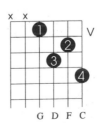

G D F C

G7♭5

G F B D♭

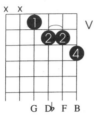

G D♭ F B   V

G7♯5

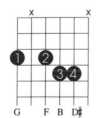

G F B D♯

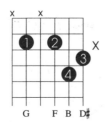

G F B D♯   X

G9

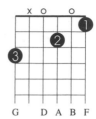

G D A B F

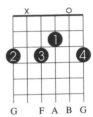

G F A B G

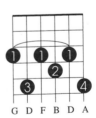

G D F B D A

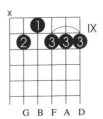

G B F A D   IX

G

G9sus4

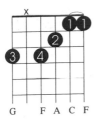

G F A C F

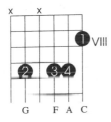

G F A C | VIII

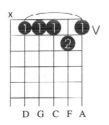

D G C F A | V

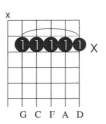

G C F A D | X

G9♭5

G B F A D♭

G B F A D♭ | IX

G9♯5

G F B D♯ A

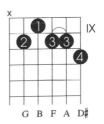

G B F A D♯ | IX

G

G13

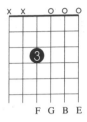

F G B E

G D F B E G

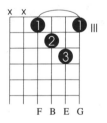

III

F B E G

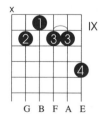

IX

G B F A E

A♭

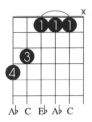

A♭ C E♭ A♭ C

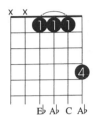

E♭ A♭ C A♭

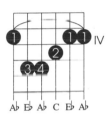

A♭ E♭ A♭ C E♭ A♭ IV

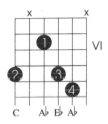

C A♭ E♭ A♭ VI

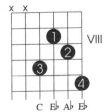

E♭ A♭ E♭ A♭ C VI

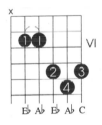

A♭ C E♭ A♭ VIII

A♭

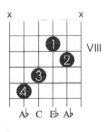

C E♭ A♭ E♭ VIII

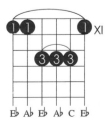

E♭ A♭ E♭ A♭ C E♭ XI

93

Absus4

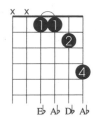

Eb Ab Db Ab

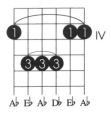

Ab Eb Ab Db Eb Ab
IV

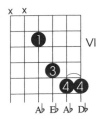

Ab Eb Ab Db
VI

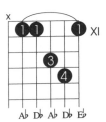

Ab Db Ab Db Eb
XI

Ab6

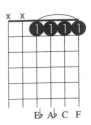

Eb Ab C F

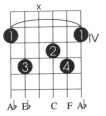

Ab Eb C F Ab
IV

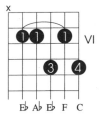

Eb Ab Eb F C
VI

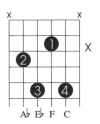

Ab Eb F C
X

94

Ab6/9

Ab C F Bb Eb

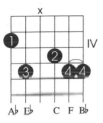

Ab Eb C F Bb — IV

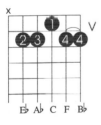

Eb Ab C F Bb — V

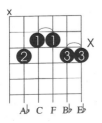

Ab C F Bb Eb — X

Abmaj7

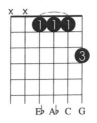

Eb Ab C G

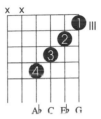

Ab C Eb G — III

Ab Eb G C Eb Ab — IV

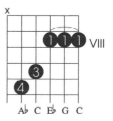

Ab C Eb G C — VIII

Ab

Abmaj9

Ab C G Bb Eb

C Ab Bb Eb G — III

Abmaj13

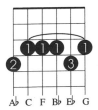

Ab C F Bb Eb G

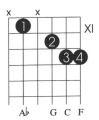

Ab G C F — XI

Abm

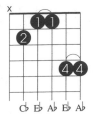

Cb Eb Ab Eb Ab

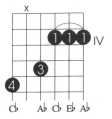

Cb Ab Cb Eb Ab — IV

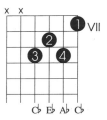

Cb Eb Ab Cb — VII

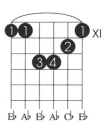

Eb Ab Eb Ab Cb Eb — XI

A♭m

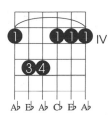

A♭ E♭ A♭ C♭ E♭ A♭   IV

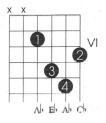

A♭ E♭ A♭ C♭   VI

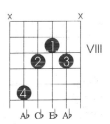

A♭ C♭ E♭ A♭   VIII

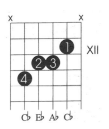

C♭ E♭ A♭ C♭   XII

A♭m6

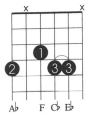

A♭ F C♭ E♭

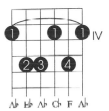

A♭ E♭ A♭ C♭ F A♭   IV

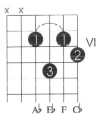

A♭ E♭ F C♭   VI

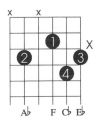

A♭ F C♭ E♭   X

A♭

A♭m7

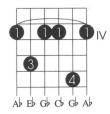

A♭ E♭ G♭ C♭ G♭ A♭

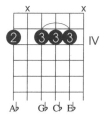

A♭ G♭ C♭ E♭

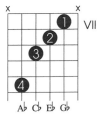

A♭ C♭ E♭ G♭

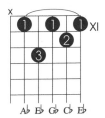

A♭ E♭ G♭ C♭ E♭

A♭m(maj7)

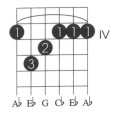

A♭ E♭ G C♭ E♭ A♭

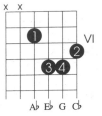

A♭ E♭ G C♭

A♭m9

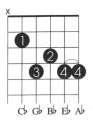

C♭ G♭ B♭ E♭ A♭

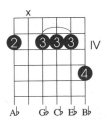

A♭ G♭ C♭ E♭ B♭

A♭

Abm11

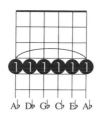

Ab Db Gb Cb Eb Ab

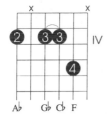

Ab Db Gb Cb Fb

Abm7b5

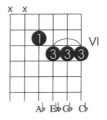

Ab Eb Gb Cb

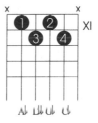

Ab Gb Cb Fb

Abm13

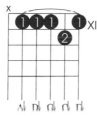

Ab Gb Cb F

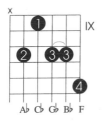

Ab Cb Gb Bb F

Ab°7

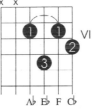

Ab Eb F Cb

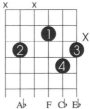

Ab F Cb Eb

Ab

A♭7

x x
1 1 1
2
E♭ A♭ C G♭

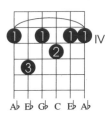

1 1 1 1 IV
2
3
A♭ E♭ G♭ C E♭ A♭

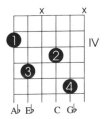

x x
1
2
3
4 IV
A♭ E♭ C G♭

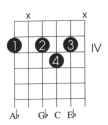

x x
1 2 3 IV
4
A♭ G♭ C E♭

A♭7

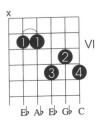

x
1 1 VI
2
3 4
E♭ A♭ E♭ G♭ C

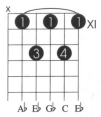

x
1 1 1 XI
3 4
A♭ E♭ G♭ C E♭

A♭7sus4

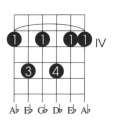

x x
1 1
3 3
E♭ A♭ D♭ G♭

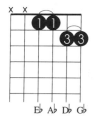

1 1 1 1 IV
3 4
A♭ E♭ G♭ D♭ E♭ A♭

100

A♭7♭5

A♭   G♭ C E♭♭

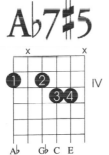

VI

A♭ E♭♭ G♭ C

A♭7♯5

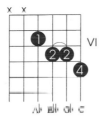

IV

A♭ G♭ C E

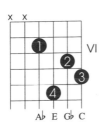

VI

A♭ E G♭ C

A♭9

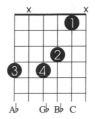

A♭   G♭ B♭ C

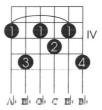

IV

A♭ E♭ G♭ C E♭ B♭

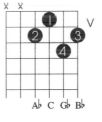

V

A♭ C G♭ B♭

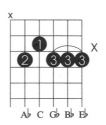

X

A♭ C G♭ B♭ E♭

A♭

Ab9sus4

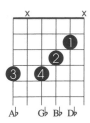

Ab Gb Bb Db

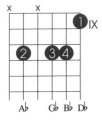

Ab Gb Bb Db

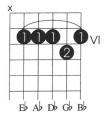

Eb Ab Db Gb Bb

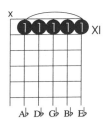

Ab Db Gb Bb Eb

Ab9b5

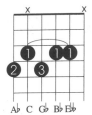

Ab C Gb Bb Ebb

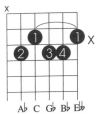

Ab C Gb Bb Ebb

Ab9#5

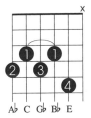

Ab C Gb Bb E

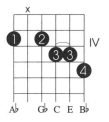

Ab Gb C E Bb

A♭13

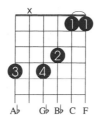

Ab Gb Bb C F

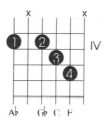

IV

Ab Gb C F

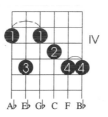

IV

Ab Eb Gb C F Bb

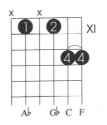

XI

Ab Gb C F

A

E A E A C# E

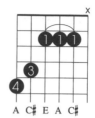

A C# E A C#

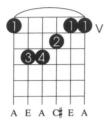

A E A C# E A

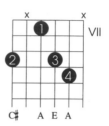

C# A E A

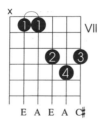

E A E A C#

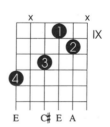

E C# E A

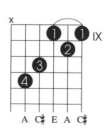

A C# E A C#

E A E A C# E

104

A6

Asus4

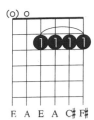

E A E A C# F#

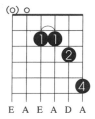

E A E A D A

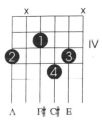

IV

A F# C# E

V

A E A D E A

V

A E C# F# A

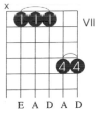

VII

E A D A D

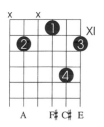

XI

A F# C# E

XII

E A D A D E

105

A6/9

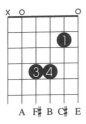

A F# B C# E

A B E A C# F#

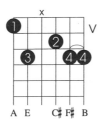

A E C# F# B

V

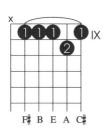

F# B E A C#

IX

Amaj7

E A E G# C# E

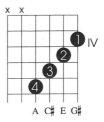

E A E A C# G#

A C# E G#

IV

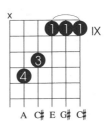

A C# E G# C#

IX

A

106

Amaj9

A E B C# G#

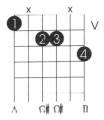

A G# C# D

Amaj13

E A E G# C# F#

A C# F# B E G#

Am

E A E A C E

A E A C E A

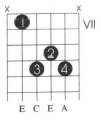

E C E A

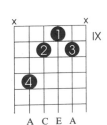

A C E A

Am

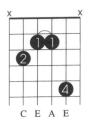

C E A E

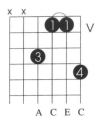

V

A C E C

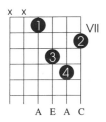

VII

A E A C

XII

E A E A C E

Am6

(o) o

E A E A C F#

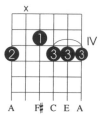

IV

A F# C E A

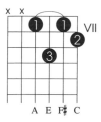

VII

A E F# C

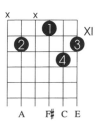

XI

A F# C E

Am7

A E G C E

A E G C G A

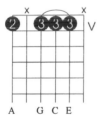

A G C E

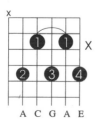

A C G A E

Am(maj7)

E A E A C G#

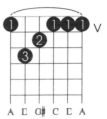

A E C# C E A

Am9

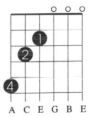

A C E G B E

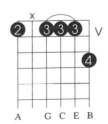

A G C E B

A

109

Am11

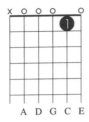

A D G C E

VII

E A D G C

Am13

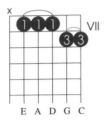

A E G C F#

V

A E G C F# A

Am7♭5

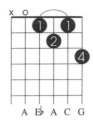

A E♭ A C G

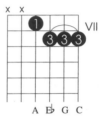

VII

A E♭ G C

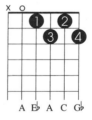

A E♭ A C G♭

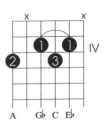

IV

A G♭ C E♭

110

A7

E A E G C# E

E A E A C# G

A E G C# E A

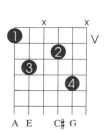

A E   C# G

A7

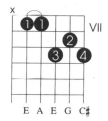

VII

E A E G C#

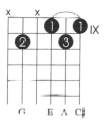

IX

G   E A C#

A7sus4

E A E A D G

V

A E G D E A

111

A7♭5

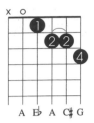

A E♭ A C♯ G

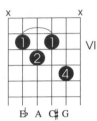

VI

E♭ A C♯ G

A7♯5

V

A   G C♯ E♯

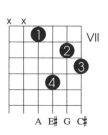

VII

A E♯ G C♯

A9

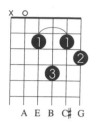

A E B C♯ G

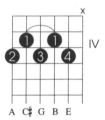

IV

A C♯ G B E

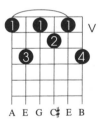

V

A E G C♯ E B

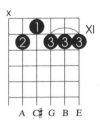

XI

A C♯ G B E

A9sus4

x   x

A   G B D

x   x

X

A   G B D

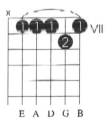

x

VII

E A D G B

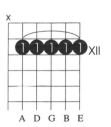

x

XII

A D G B E

A9b5

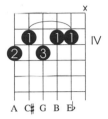

x

IV

A C# G B Eb

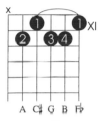

x

XI

A C# G B Fb

A9#5

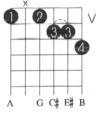

x

V

A   G C# E# B

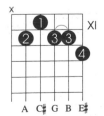

x

XI

A C# G B E#

A

113

A13

A E G C# F#

A G A C# F#

A E G C# F# A

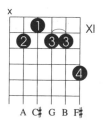

A C# G B F#

B♭

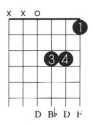

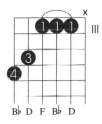

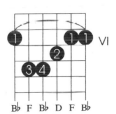

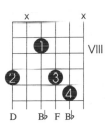

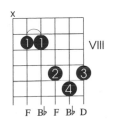

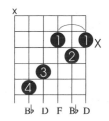

B♭sus4

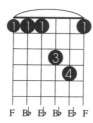

F B♭ E♭ E♭ E♭ F

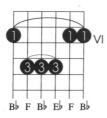

B♭ F B♭ E♭ F B♭   VI

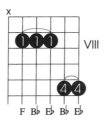

x   F B♭ E♭ B♭ E♭   VIII

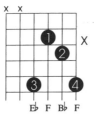

x x   E♭ F B♭ F   X

B♭6

x   B♭ F B♭ D G

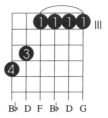

B♭ D F B♭ D G   III

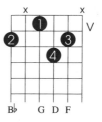

x   x   B♭   G D F   V

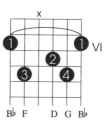

x   B♭ F   D G B♭   VI

B♭

116

Bb6/9   Bbmaj7

Bb D G C F

Bb F A D F

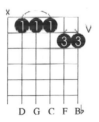
III

Bb C F Bb D G

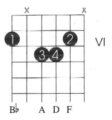
V

Bb D F A

V

D G C F Bb

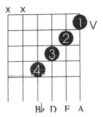
VI

Bb A D F

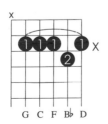
X

G C F Bb D

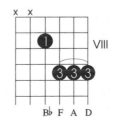
VIII

Bb F A D

117

B♭maj9

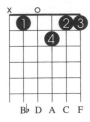

B♭ D A C F

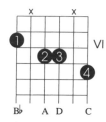

VI

B♭ A D C

B♭maj13

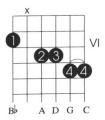

B♭ A D G

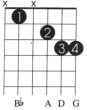

VI

B♭ A D G C

B♭m

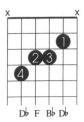

D♭ F B♭ D♭

III

F D♭ F B♭

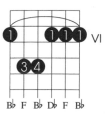

VI

B♭ F B♭ D♭ F B♭

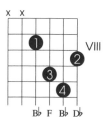

VIII

B♭ F B♭ D♭

B♭

118

B♭m   B♭m6

F B♭ F B♭ D♭ F

B♭ F G D♭

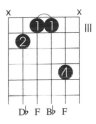

III

D♭ F B♭ F

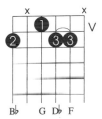

V

B♭   G D♭ F

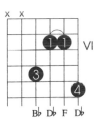

VI

B♭ D♭ F D♭

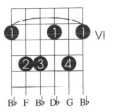

VI

B♭ F B♭ D♭ G B♭

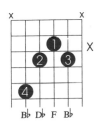

X

B♭ D♭ F B♭

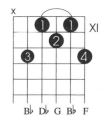

XI

B♭ D♭ G B♭ F

B♭

119

B♭m7

F B♭ F A♭ D♭ F

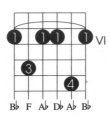

B♭ F A♭ D♭ A♭ B♭

VI

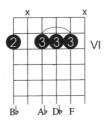

B♭ A♭ D♭ F

VI

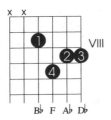

B♭ F A♭ D♭

VIII

B♭m(maj7)

B♭ F A D♭ F

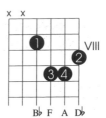

B♭ F A D♭

VIII

B♭m9

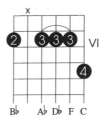

B♭ A♭ D♭ F C

VI

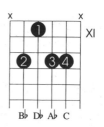

B♭ D♭ A♭ C

XI

B♭

B♭m11

B♭ E♭ A♭ D♭ F

VIII

F B♭ E♭ A♭ D♭

B♭m7♭5

B♭ A♭ D♭ F♭

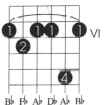

VI

B♭ F♭ A♭ D♭ A♭ B♭

B♭m13

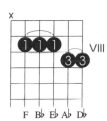

B♭ A♭ D♭ G

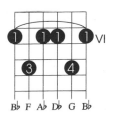

VI

B♭ F A♭ D♭ G B♭

B♭°7

B♭ F♭ A♭♭ D♭

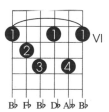

VI

B♭ F♭ B♭ D♭ A♭♭ B♭

B♭

B♭7

B♭ F A♭ D F

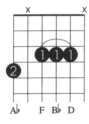

A♭ F B♭ D

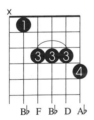

B♭ F B♭ D A♭

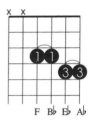

B♭ F A♭ D F B♭

B♭7

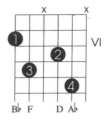

VI

B♭ F D A♭

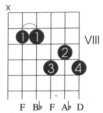

VIII

F B♭ F A♭ D

B♭7sus4

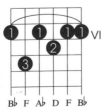

F B♭ E♭ A♭

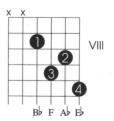

VIII

B♭ F A♭ E♭

B♭

Bb7b5

Bb D Ab D Fb

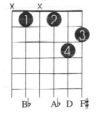

Bb Fb Ab D — VIII

Bb7#5

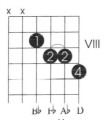

Bb Ab D F#

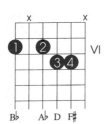

Bb Ab D F# — VI

Bb9

Bb D Ab C F

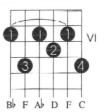

Bb Ab C D — III

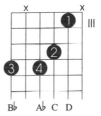

Bb F Ab D F C — VI

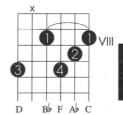

D Bb F Ab C — VIII

Bb

Bb9sus4

Bb Eb Ab C F

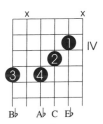

VI

Bb F Ab Eb F C

IV

Bb Ab C Eb

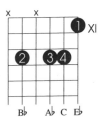

XI

Bb Ab C Eb

Bb9b5

Bb D Ab C Fb

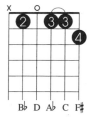

V

D Ab C Fb Bb

Bb9#5

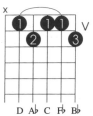

Bb D Ab C F#

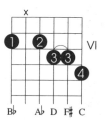

VI

Bb Ab D F# C

Bb

124

Bb13

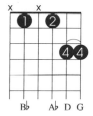

B♭   A♭ D G

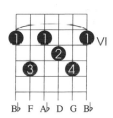

VI

B♭ F A♭ D G B♭

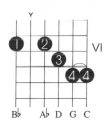

VI

B♭   A♭ D G C

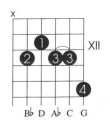

XII

B♭ D A♭ C G

125

B

F♯ B F♯ B D♯ F♯

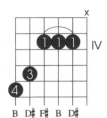

IV

B D♯ F♯ B D♯

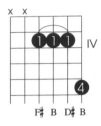

IV

F♯ B D♯ B

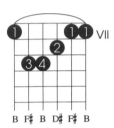

VII

B F♯ B D♯ F♯ B

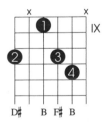

IX

D♯ B F♯ B

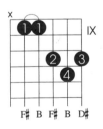

IX

F♯ B F♯ B D♯

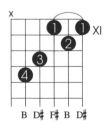

XI

B D♯ F♯ B D♯

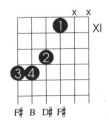

XI

F♯ B D♯ F♯

Bsus4　　B6

F# B E B E F#

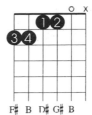

F# B D# G# B

B F# B E F# B

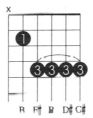

B F# B D# C#

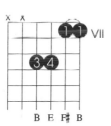

B E F# B

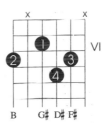

B G# D# F#

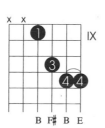

B F# B E

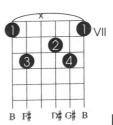

B F# D# G# B

B

B6/9

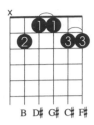

B D# G# C# F#

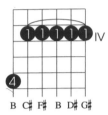

B C# F# B D# G#

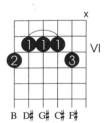

B D# G# C# F#

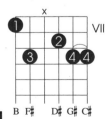

B F# D# G# C#

Bmaj7

F# B D# A# B

F# B F# A# D# F#

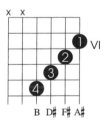

B D# F# A#

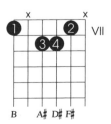

B A# D# F#

128

Bmaj9

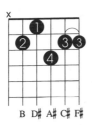

B D# A# C# F#

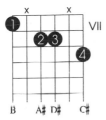

VII

B   A# D#   C#

Bmaj9

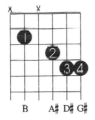

B   A# D# G#

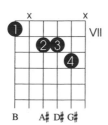

VII

B   A# D# G#

Bm

D B D F#

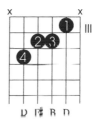

III

D F# B D

VII

B F# B D F# B

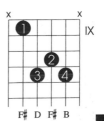

IX

F# D F# B

B

Bm

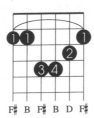

F♯ B F♯ B D F♯

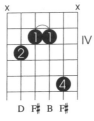

D F♯ B F♯ — IV

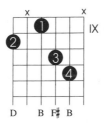

D B F♯ B — IX

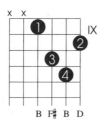

B F♯ B D — IX

Bm6

B G♯ D F♯

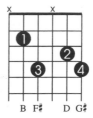

B F♯ D G♯

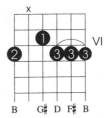

B G♯ D F♯ B — VI

B F♯ B D G♯ B — VII

B

130

Bm7

B D A B F#

B F# A D F#

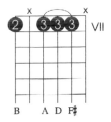

VII

B   A D F#

VII

B F# A D A B

Bm(maj7)

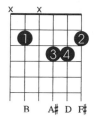

B   A# D F#

VII

B F# A# D F# B

Bm9

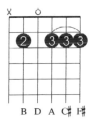

B D A C# F#

VII

B   A D F# C#

131

Bm11

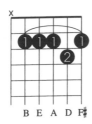

B E A D F#

B E A D F# B — VII

Bm7b5

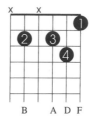

B A D F

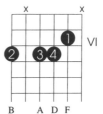

B A D F — VI

Bm13

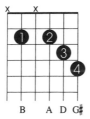

B A D G#

B F# A D G# B — VII

B°7

B F Ab D

B F B D Ab B — VII

B

132

B7

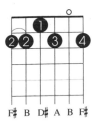

F♯ B D♯ A B F♯

B F♯ B D♯ A

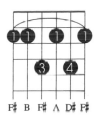

F♯ B F♯ A D♯ F♯

B F♯ A D♯ F♯ B

B7

VII

B F♯ A D♯ A B

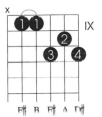

IX

F♯ B D♯ A D♯

B7sus4

F♯ B D♯ A E F♯

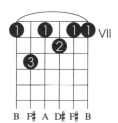

VII

B F♯ A E F♯ B

B7♭5

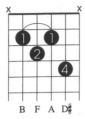

B F A D♯

VII

B F A D♯

B7♯5

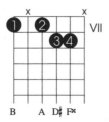

B D♯ A B F𝄪

VII

B A D♯ F𝄪

B9

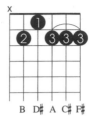

B D♯ A C♯ F♯

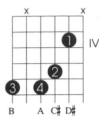
IV

B A C♯ D♯

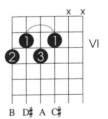
VI

B D♯ A C♯

VII

B F♯ A D♯ F♯ C♯

B9sus4

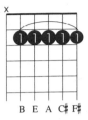

B E A C# F#

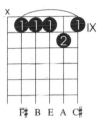

IX

F# B E A C#

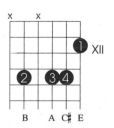

V

B   A C# E

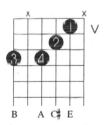

XII

B   A C# E

B9b5

B D# A C# F

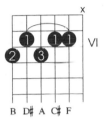

VI

B D# A C# F

B9#5

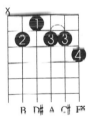

B D# A C# F※

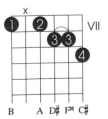

VII

B   A D# F※ C#

135

B13

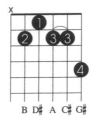

B D♯ A C♯ G♯

B A D♯ G♯

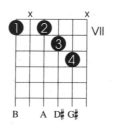

VII

B A D♯ G♯

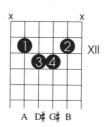

XII

A D♯ G♯ B

B

Barre, Power, Suspended, Slash, Alternative, Classic and Other Chords

Barre Chords

Barre chords are so-called because one of the fretting hand's fingers is pressed against two or more strings (this is shown as a curved line in the fretbox).

They can be moved up or down the neck to different fret positions to create new chords. The advantage of this is that once you've learned one new barre shape, you've in effect learned 12 new chords!

Opposite are diagrams showing the names of the notes on the sixth and fifth strings. To find any barre chord, look at the fretbox to see whether the root note (shown in a black circle) appears on the fifth or sixth string, then move the barre shape up or down until you reach the desired pitch. For example, a chord of Ab, (also known as G#) can be played using an 'F shape' moved up to the 4th fret.

The first diagram shows you how to find any barre chord position, and will help you if the chord you want has a sharp (#) in its name.

Use the second diagram if the chord you want has a flat (b) in its name.

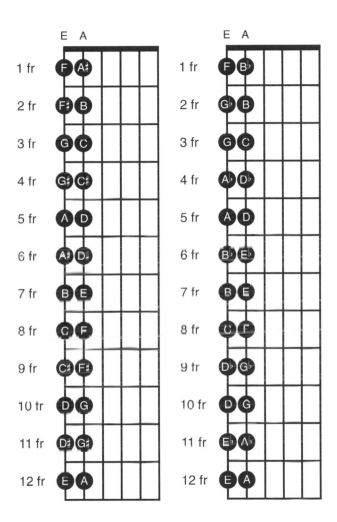

F

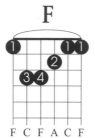

F C F A C F

The F barre shape has its root on the sixth string. Move it up one fret and you get F♯, up two and you get G. You can even play it way up at the 12th fret to create a barre chord of E.

B♭

B♭ F B♭ D F

Any B♭-based shape has its root on the fifth string. Sometimes, if you're changing chords quickly, it's easier to change between the F and B♭ shapes because it involves less hand movement.

B♭ "lazy" version

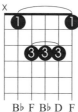

B♭ F B♭ D F

Lots of rock players favour this version of B♭– it sounds nearly as full, and is far easier to play. Make sure that you don't flatten the third finger all the way over.

Fm

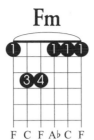

F C F A♭ C F

For this, the same principle applies as for the F major shape – move it up one fret and you get F#m, move it up one more and you get Gm, and so on all the way up to Em at the 12th fret.

B♭m

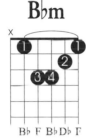

B♭ F B♭ D♭ F

This minor shape has its root on the 5th string, so you could create a chord of Bm if played at the 2nd fret, Cm at the third etc. Its sweet tone makes it especially good for funk, jazz and dance music.

F7

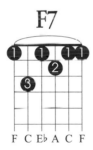

F C E♭ A C F

Although this barre version of F7 looks very similar to the ordinary barre F shape, it's quite difficult to make that barred fourth string sound clearly in the middle of the chord.

F7 (version 2)

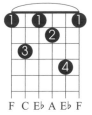

F C Eb A Eb F

Add your little finger to the chord and you get this more colourful-sounding version of F7. It's a tricky stretch though, so ensure that all of the notes sound clearly as you strum across it.

Bb7

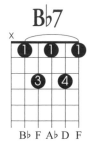

Bb F Ab D F

This is a barre version of the ordinary open A7 shape. Note that the root is on the fifth string. This means that there's a chord of B7 at the 2nd fret, C7 at the 3rd, and A7 up at the 12th.

Fmaj7

F C E A C F

Many players like to omit the first string when they play this chord because it clashes a bit with the note on the fourth string. Like all the other chords in this section, it can be moved to any fret.

B♭maj7

B♭ F A D F

This version of the major seventh barre chord is more common, and sounds 'sweeter' than the Fmaj7 opposite. Note that the barre doesn't have to press all the strings – just the fifth and first.

Fm7

F C E♭ A♭ C F

Another six-string chord, this time with a barre covering all but one of the strings. Some funk players choose a 'partial chord' version, just using the first finger flattened over the first three strings. (see p157)

B♭m7

B♭ F A♭ D♭ F

This versatile chord shape sounds just as good at the 13th fret as it does at the 1st. Try sliding into it as you strum rhythmic patterns for a funky 70s disco sound.

Power chords

Power chords (also called '5' chords) are the sound behind almost every rock and metal band ever, from Black Sabbath to Metallica. They have a strident, aggressive feel, and sound good with lots of distortion. As with the barre chords in the previous section, the F and B♭ versions of the chords can be moved up to any fret using the fingerboard diagrams on page 139. However, there are some great examples which feature open strings which are included here too. Power chords are also useful for making up your own rock riffs – try moving the chord around the neck while you play downstrokes on the bass strings with your plectrum.

F5

F C F

With this moveable power chord there are two choices – either play the three bass strings as shown, or only hit the sixth and fifth strings. Remember to mute the other three strings.

B♭5

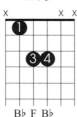

B♭ F B♭

Sometimes you may not need to move the F5 shape all over the neck – there may be a version of the power chord you want with its root on the fifth string.

A5

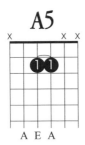

A E A

This open power chord appears at the beginning of 'Won't Get Fooled Again' by The Who, 'Tie Your Mother Down' by Queen, plus many a pub blues standard. It's a stripped-down version of A major.

A5 (version 2)

A E A E A

This version of A5 covers three octaves, so it has an even more powerful sound. If you have trouble stretching the little finger over two strings, do persevere – the effort will be worth it.

C5

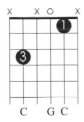

C G C

Although this is not a commonly-used shape, it's interesting because it uses muting techniques to stop some strings from sounding. Famously used in ZZ Top's 'Gimme All Your Lovin''.

D5

D A D

Like the open A5 on page 145, this is just a simplified version of the equivalent major chord. You might find, though, that a fretted version (Bb5 shape at the 5th fret) sounds more convincing.

D5 (version 2)

D A D A

Here's a more spaced-out version of the same chord. Try adding distortion and delay, then pick across the strings one at a time for a typical rock anthem intro.

E5

E B E

This is the lowest, thickest-sounding power chord anywhere on the fingerboard. It sounds great played with downstrokes as a rock or blues accompaniment part.

E5 (version 2)

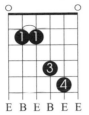

E B E B E E

This is an expanded version of the more common three string version. The first and second strings can be played open for a more 'jangly' sound.

F5 (version 2)

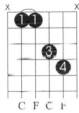

C F C F

III Although this version of F5 is moveable, its root is actually on the fourth string. So it creates G5 when played at the 5th fret, Ab5 at the 6th, and D5 way up at the 12th.

G5

G D G D G

If you omit the 5th string from the easy G major chord shown on page 82, you get this powerful alternative to a G5 barre shape. Use the side of the second finger to mute the 5th string.

Suspended chords

Suspended chords are so-called because one of the notes has been taken out and replaced with a different note which isn't part of a major or minor chord – so a note is 'suspended'. They have an unfinished, suspended-in-space sound to them. Sus chords, as they're known, come in two types – sus2 and sus4, of which sus4 is the most common. They are rarely used on their own, because of their incomplete sound they nearly always resolve to a more straightforward chord. Check out the strummed chords at the end of The Beatles' 'You've Got To Hide Your Love Away', or The Who's 'Pinball Wizard'.

Fsus4

F C F Bb C F

This is the standard six-string sus4 with its root on the sixth string. As with all F type barre chords, it can be moved to any fret position using the fingerboard diagrams on page 139.

Bbsus4

Bb F Bb Eb F

The other moveable sus4 shape has its root on the fifth string. Slide the little finger back one fret and you've got an ordinary Bb barre shape, making the change from sus4 to major chord really easy.

B♭sus2

B♭ F B♭ C F

If you play this moveable sus2 barre shape at the 6th fret, that's the intro chord from 'Don't Dream It's Over' by Crowded House. Resolve this shape to a major chord by simply adding the little finger.

Asus2

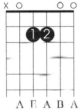

A E A B A

Much beloved of acoustic-playing songwriters, Asus2 sounds more complicated and difficult than it really is. Try making up riffs using combinations of A, Asus4 and Asus2.

Asus4

A E A D A

If you're playing a song that starts on a chord of D, wait until you get to a chord of A in the music, and try playing Asus4, followed by A. This is called resolution and is a useful songwriting tool.

Bsus4

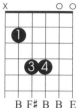

B F♯ B B E

The note of B (at the 4th fret, third string) is doubled by the open second string, creating a 12-string guitar effect. This shape appears in Suzanne Vega's 'Luka'.

Csus4

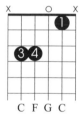

C F G C

As long as you only play the middle four strings, this is a much easier alternative than the barre shape Csus4 at the 3rd fret. If you use this fingering, it's easy to resolve to a normal C chord.

Dsus2

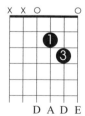

D A D E

Play a D chord and take one finger off to create the chord of Dsus2. John Lennon used a combination of sus2, major, and sus4 chords like this to write 'Happy Xmas (War Is Over)'.

Dsus4

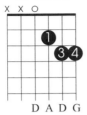

D A D G

Many players like to keep their second finger at the 2nd fret on the first string, in readiness for changing the Dsus4 back to a D.

Esus4

E B E A B E

A similar idea can apply to Esus4, which resolves easily to a straight chord of E. Bear in mind, though, that including the open third string creates a chord of Em, not Esus2.

Gsus4

G D G C G

This less-used open sus4 chord is most useful if you're playing it on an acoustic, because it uses two open strings in the middle of the chord. Playing the first string is optional.

Other useful open chords

Sometimes a particular shape or fingering might create a chord with a complex-sounding name, even if it's really easy to play. Shown here are some of the common examples you may see in songbooks. These shapes are particularly good for acoustic songwriting because they sound colourful and complex, helping to suggest melodies and ideas. All of these examples contain at least one open string, and none of them use barres.

You may notice that most of these examples are familiar chords with one or more of the notes replaced by an open string. You can apply this idea to almost any chord you know: experiment and see what happens.

Aadd9

A E B C♯ E

This chord is the adaptation of the open A chord shape (see page 104), but take note of the finger number changes that are necessary to accommodate the stretch.

Cadd9

C E G D E

This is a C chord with the little finger added at the 3rd fret. It works especially well with songs that start or end on a G chord. The first open string can be omitted.

Emadd9

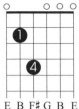

E B F# G B E

Although this chord isn't that great if you just strum it up and down, try picking across the notes one at a time for an interesting rock ballad-style intro.

Fmaj7#11

F C F A B E

Don't be put off by the jazzy-sounding name here – this is a great chord. Again, it's most effective when you pick the notes one at a time.

G6

G B D E

If you move an Fmaj7 up two frets, you get this version of G6, as used by Keith Richards in The Rolling Stones' 'Angie', and at the end of The Beatles' 'She Loves You'.

Slash chords

Many chord books and song transcriptions feature slash chords, which can confuse some guitarists because they don't know whether to play the chord on the left or the right of the slash. The first letter name refers to the chord name itself; and the second is a single bass note. If you're playing in a band, normally the guitarist would play the chord before the slash, and the bass player would play the single bass note. But if you're playing unaccompanied, you need to figure out a way to finger the chord *and* bass note.

A/G

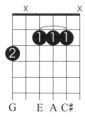

G   E A C♯

Although it's possible to play a straight A chord in the normal way and reach across with the little finger for the bass note, this version, with the first finger flattened across three strings, is much easier.

D/F♯

F♯ A D A D F♯

Although some guitar teachers may frown on the use of the thumb, many players including Jimi Hendrix and Paul Simon have used it succssfully.

G/A

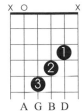

A G B D

There is no reason why the bass note shouldn't be an open string. The chord of G/A is sometimes referred to as A11, and it has a very warm, jazzy sound.

C/B

B E G C E

Here, the root of an ordinary C chord has simply been dropped down a fret. Paul Simon uses it in the acoustic rhythm part from 'America'.

D/C

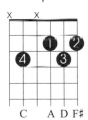

C   A D F#

As with the A/G chord, the side of the little finger is used to stop an open string from sounding. It's the second chord in the verse of The Beatles' 'Dear Prudence'.

Alternative Chord Shapes

Playing a rhythm part doesn't always mean using the shapes you'll find in the main section of this book. Lots of pro players use less conventional shapes, either because they work better in the context of a band mix; because they're more convenient to play at the time; or simply because they prefer the sound. Here are two moveable chord shapes not normally mentioned in regular chord books, and three examples of 'partial chords'.

D7 'Middle D7'

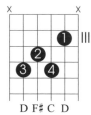

D F♯ C D

So-called because it doesn't use the outer two strings, this fretted shape is handy in many different styles, though it's perhaps most common in Rock and Roll or Rhythm & Blues.

D 'Folky C shape'

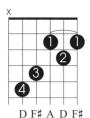

D F♯ A D F♯

If you look carefully you'll notice that this is just a C chord moved up two frets, with a barre over the first three strings. Many players actually prefer this version to a conventional barre chord shape.

F (partial)

X X X

A C F

The simplest way to create a partial chord is to look at any chord you already know – and don't play all of the notes. This is a chord of F with some of the lower notes removed.

Dm (partial)

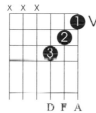

X X X

V

D F A

This chord is based on a Dm barre at the 5th fret, but because you're not playing any of the bass notes, you don't need the barre. Try playing this shape while somebody else plays an ordinary Dm.

A7 (partial)

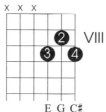

X X X

VIII

E G C♯

Although this isn't based on a conventional barre chord, it's still a valid seventh chord shape – it's basically an open D7 chord (see page 34), moved up 7 frets.

Classic Chords

There is a small number of chords that have become classics in their own right because they've become instantly recognisable. The fourteen examples shown here have all been associated with a particular song, and some have been the subject of much debate among guitarists as to how they should be played!

Each of them should be identifiable if you just strum across the whole chord once, with the exception of the Chuck Berry example.

G7sus4 'A Hard Day's Night'

G D F C D G

Not *exactly* what was played on the original recording (there were two guitars, a high G from Paul McCartney's bass, and a chord from George Martin's piano), but arranged for one guitar it sounds fine.

Dm7add11 'Walking On The Moon'

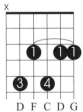

D F C D G

This Police song would not have been complete without the 'chang' of this great-sounding chord on Andy Summers' Fender Telecaster. Add a C barre chord and you can play along with the bass riff.

Em^{maj9} '007'

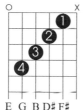

E G B D♯ F♯

The James Bond Theme ends with this ominous-sounding chord, played in 1960 by session guitarist Vic Flick. Use the side of the fretting hand's first finger to mute the first string.

E7♯9 The 'Hendrix' chord

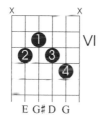

VI

E G♯ D G

'Foxy Lady', 'Purple Haze', 'Voodoo Chile'... All three of these Jimi Hendrix classics have featured this chord. The open first and sixth strings are optional in each case, making the chord sound fuller.

D(♯5) 'No Particular Place To Go'

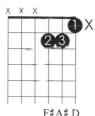

F♯ A♯ D

This partial chord, played up and down rapidly a total of 13 times, forms the intro to Chuck Berry's famous rock 'n' roll tune.

Cmaj7 'A Design For Life'

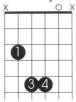

C G C B

Pick across the strings one by one, starting on the root note, until you get to the second string, then pick back in the other direction. It's the first part of the Manic Street Preachers' 'A Design For Life'.

D & Dsus4 'Crazy Little Thing Called Love'

D A D F#/G

Play a normal D chord, then add and remove the little finger (4) while you're strumming. That's the intro to this Queen single, from their 1980 album, *The Game*.

E/D 'Hole Hearted'

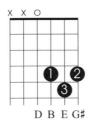

D B E G#

Play a D chord twice, then slide it up two frets and pick the strings one by one. Nuno Bettencourt plays this on an acoustic just before the verse section from Extreme's hit 'Hole Hearted'.

E5 'Paranoid'

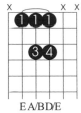

VII Because of the partial barre behind two of the fretted notes, you can play hammer-ons between the 7th and 9th fret, as Tony Iommi does in the intro from this early Black Sabbath recording.

E A/BD/E

E9 'James Brown'

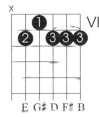

VI This funky ninth chord shape appears in a long list of James Brown tunes, and is one the most commonly used chords in 70s funk and disco. Try sliding up to the chord as you strum rapidly

E G♯ D F♯ B

B & Bsus4 'Pinball Wizard'

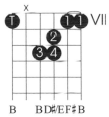

VII You need to reach the thumb over the top of the neck to reach the bass note here. Use fast up and down strums while you add and remove the little finger note at the 9th fret.

B   BD♯/EF♯B

C♯add9 'Message In A Bottle'

C♯ G♯ D♯

IV Here's another chord from a Police track. Most of the time, when add9 type chords appear in a song, they're picked one note at a time rather than strummed right across.

D/A 'All Right Now'

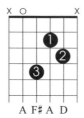

A F♯ A D

The D/A shape is played after a regular A chord in Paul Kossoff's rhythm guitar part from this track by 70s rock-blues band Free. It also appears in Queen's 'Hammer To Fall.'

Fsus2 'Live Forever'

F G C G

At the end of the chorus from this early Oasis hit, Noel Gallagher cranks up the distortion levels as he picks out a riff using the notes from this open chord shape.

Alternative Tunings

Drop D (DADBGE)

Simply detune your low E string one whole tone, so it's an octave lower than your D string. Power chords are much easier (and fun) to play with this tuning.

D5

G5

A5

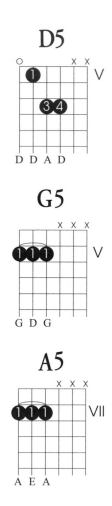

Double Drop D (DADBGD)

Now detune your other E string one whole tone, so it matches
your 4th and your 6th string. Bob Dylan used this tuning in 'The
Ballad of Hollis Brown' from his 1964 album, *The Times They Are
A-Changin'*.

D5

D A D A D D

Dsus4

D A D G D D

Aadd11

A E A C#D

Open D (DADF#AD)

Open D (and Open E) tunings are two of the traditional open major chord tunings. Try playing with a slide for an authentic blues sound.

E

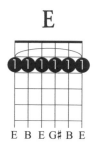

E B E G# B E

Dm7

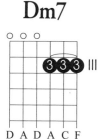

D A D A C F

A7 (no 3rd)

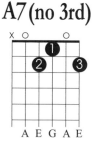

A E G A E

Open E (EBEG#BE)

Open E is exactly the same as Open D, but tuned up a tone. You may want to use a capo on the 2nd fret, in Open D, instead of tuning the strings above their normal pitch. Joni Mitchell utilised this tuning on her 1970 hit, 'Big Yellow Taxi'.

E

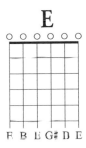

E B G# D E

Emaj7

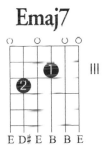

E D# E B B E

A9/E

E C# E A B E

DADGAD

Technically an open Dsus4 chord – known also Modal D or just
DADGAD; used to great effect by Led Zeppelin's Jimmy Page,
firstly on 'Black Mountain Side', and later, 'Kashmir'.

D5

D A D A A D

Gadd9

G D G B A D

Aadd9/11

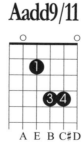

A E B C♯ D

Open G (DGDGBD)

Like the other open tunings, this sounds great with a slide. Try a capo on the 3rd fret, to emulate Dire Straits' 'Romeo And Juliet'.

D

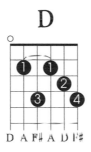

D A F♯ A D F♯

C

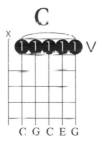

C G C E G

G7

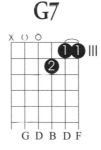

G D B D F

Open C6 (CACGCE)

This tuning gives a rich sound often with very little fingering. 'Little Lion Man' (Mumford And Sons) and 'Bron-Yr-Aur' (Led Zeppelin) both use this particular tuning.

C

C C C G C E

Fmaj9

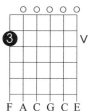

F A C G C E

Am7

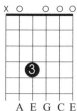

A E G C E

CGCDGA

The CGCDGA tuning has been used extensively by Martin Carthy; the combination of 2nd and 5th intervals help give the chords a distinct flavour.

G

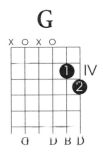

Cmaj7

Am7

CGCFCE

Nick Drake used this tuning a lot, especially on his 1970 album, *Pink Moon*. If you don't want to tune up your B string, try tuning everything a semitone flat.

C

C G C G C E

Dm9

D A D F C E

G5

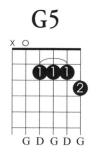

G D G D G

CGDAEG

Probably the most unusual tuning in this collection, (otherwise known as New Standard Tuning), this was devised by Robert Fripp in 1985. You may want to change your top two strings to a higher gauge to prevent your strings snapping.

C

C G E C E G

G

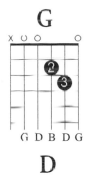

G D B D G

D

D A D A F♯ A

Try creating a few chords of your own!

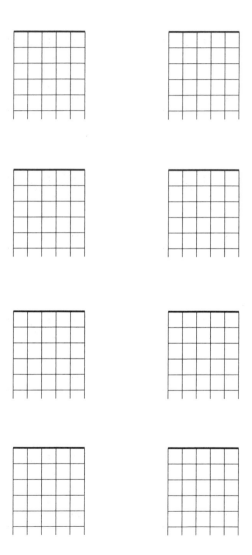

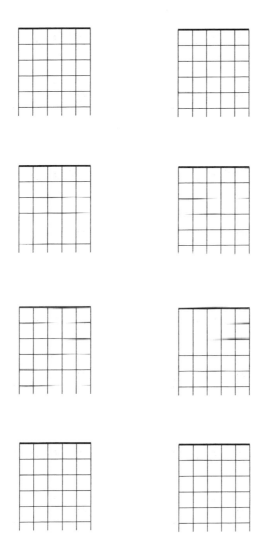